Birthing *Your* Destiny

LINDA DOROTHY TALLEY

Passion Publications

Published by Passion Publications
A division of Tell The Truth International
7005 Woodbine Ave
Sacramento, Ca. 95822
passionbookpub@gmail.com

Printed in the United States of America

*All scriptures are from the KJV Bible
version unless stated otherwise.*

Cover image and design by:
Charlyn_design@fiverr.com

Illustrations by Beni Sultan

ISBN: 9781957101-09-5 (paperback)
ISBN: 9781957101-10-1 (ebook)

CONTENTS

DEDICATION

This book is dedicated to my Beloved Dear parents, Bishop Grover L. Talley and Evangelist Helen Talley, two wonderful God-fearing souls who taught their 12 children to love God, how to praise and depend upon God and have faith in God. They dedicated their lives to the building of God's Kingdom, starting with their children and then a church ministry where they faithfully pastored until the Lord called them home.

I also dedicate this book to the 5 children that God gave me to birth and raise, Raphael (deceased), Crystal, Tiffany, Shaun, and Travonte, and to the countless others of whom I did not birth. It is to each of you I say: Know God! Seek Him with your whole heart, your mind, body, and strength. Know He is a rewarder of those who diligently seek

Him. My beloved, your destiny is within. May the following pages provide the path for which to reach it. In Jesus' matchless name, Amen.

Lots of Love and Thanks for the Inspiration, Encouragement, Prayers, the "You Can Do It," the Pushing, and Sharing Your Gifts of Wisdom and Knowledge as well; to Minister Keven Eldridge (adopted son), Dr. Kathryn Taylor (niece), and Pastor Benjamin Marshall (nephew).

My mother told me when I was about 5 or 6 years old, I told her I was going to be a nurse. I didn't know what such a proclamation entailed. All I know is that the desire was so strong and that's what I had to be, a nurse. I didn't know what a nurse was. We never visited a hospital or any doctor for that matter unless a family member was seriously ill.

We never had a television. Being a large family growing up during the 1950s, we had limited resources. We had no access to healthcare or upward mobility economically. Besides being a pastor, my father was also a barber. My mother worked as a housekeeper, then a childcare provider for children with special needs. While we didn't have much, we were blessed to grow our own vegetables, raise our meats, milk the goats and cow, churn our butter, and can our fruit. If any of us got sick, my mother was the doctor. Any wounds we suffered she would clean and apply blessed oil, pray for it, and bandaged it.

I remember once, while playing outdoors my brother Jack, 10 years old at the time, fell on the porch steps and hit his forehead very hard. The right eye was knocked out of the socket. For three days my mother filled the open socket with blessed oil and prayed. The eye, which could not be seen for two days, after the third day, his eye began to come forward and his sight was restored. Even today, at the age of 81 years old at this time, my brother Jack has 20/20 vision today- a miracle.

Years later, I recall my mother retelling this story to a visitor. Knowing that Mother Talley was a woman of God, the visitor was amazed while also kindly stating, "That was the most dangerous thing you could do, putting oil in the eye." My mother didn't flinch or appear to second guess what she had done for the kind of faith she had. When she prayed, God answered every time.

By the age of twenty, I was working as a Licensed Vocational Nurse. I then pursued more education, receiving an Associates of Arts and Sciences, then a Bachelors of Nursing and Public Health Nurse (PHN).

In 1996, after working so many all-night shifts for years as a labor and delivery nurse, God suddenly woke me up from my sleep. It was about 12 noon. He told me to get up and start writing. The clarity with which the Lord spoke to me was surreal; I had never heard His voice speak with such clarity before - this time was very different.

The Lord said, "Get a pen and paper." Baffled and confused, I could only say, "Lord, what would you have me write?" The revelation of what God gave me to write persisted for several days. Each day He would give me more to write relating to a woman giving birth. What I had not realized at that time, God had given me "Destiny". It was up to me to ensure that I gave birth to it. As God imparted to the prophet Jeremiah, he also reminded me, *"Before I formed thee in the belly, I knew thee; and before thou came forth out of the womb, I sanctified thee, and I ordained thee a prophet unto the nations."* (Jeremiah 1:5 KJV).

Sometime after I completed what God had given me to write, I began to share in women's groups, retreats, and conferences. Each time I shared, I was asked immediately following, "Do you have a book?" or they would ask if I could share my notes. This book is the fruition of the collective teachings I've shared throughout the years about **Birthing Your Destiny, Gifts, Talents, Dreams and Visions.**

INTRODUCTION

My dear sisters, it is time for birthing, travailing, and pushing. You can try to model yourself after someone you perceive to be great, but doing so cheapens the true calling that's on your life. Be the genuine. Your destiny is yours; you are an original. What is God's plan for your destiny? That which God has placed in you is uniquely yours and no one else can carry it. My desire is that women reconnect with the physical experience of pregnancy, through a spiritual birthing experience that gives life to God's plan for their lives.

The illustrations contained in this book are natural, but the principles are biblical and spiritual. By the end of our journey together, you will be transformed in mind, body, and spirit, better equipped to win in your life and in ministry. May the revelation that is unveiled to you in the following chapters help you re-examine your life, your life choices, and the plans God has for you.

There are works that you know God has given you, yet those works have lain dormant until now. I'll say it again; those works have lain dormant until now! It's time for you to remove the barren mindset that paralyzed your future. Now is the time to give birth to what God has ASSIGNED FOR YOU, PUSH!!!

Years ago, I had the opportunity to go on an Alaskan cruise for a conference and I heard something that made me want to Birth my Destiny. One of God's greatest, Pastor Myles Munroe, asked the congregation; Where is the richest place on earth? I found out it was the graveyard. People have died with all kinds of ministry, music, songs, abilities, books, gifts, recipes and the list can go on and on. They never produced or birthed their destiny. They did not function in the gift that God gave them because they let fears and others discourage them. Don't let this be you. **Right now, is the time to give birth!**

CHAPTER 1

Getting Pregnant

What a joy when you and your husband have talked about getting pregnant. Tonight, is the night, and excitement fills the air. You are happy because "I'm getting pregnant." You are preparing yourself for your husband, happy and excited, preparing your body, bathing and using your best scrubs, body lotions, and colognes. Bed covers pulled back and roses in the bed and favorite drinks chilled by the bed side.

Spiritual Conception

This concept relates to birthing your destiny, your ministry, your dreams, your gifts, and talents. Jeremiah 1:4-7 states:

> *"The word of the Lord came to me saying, Before I formed you in the womb I knew you, before you were born, I set you apart. I appointed you as a prophet to the nations; Ah, Sovereign Lord, I said, I do not know how to speak; I am only a child; But the Lord said to me, Do not say, I am only a child; You must go to everyone I send you to and say whatever I command you. Do not be afraid of them, for I am with you and I will rescue you declares the Lord."*

The Lord God knew you long before you were born or conceived. God already knows who you are. He thought about you and has a plan for you. When you feel discouraged or inadequate, remember that God has always thought of you as valuable and that He has a purpose in mind for you.

It's time for birthing. You're asking what is my destiny, my gift, my calling? Some people think ministry is just standing behind a pulpit, but there are many types of ministries and gifts, and you'll find that in First Corinthians the 12th and the 14th chapter. Examples of these gifts include: apostle, prophet, teachers, healing, discernment, helps, government, motivational speaking, and many other things.

You can't be like your favorite speaker, teacher, preacher, or singer. You want to be an original. Did you know that whatever you were going to be was imparted unto you the day God saved you or before you were conceived or while you were in your mother's womb? You must ask God: "Lord, mold me, wash me, anoint me for Your service."

You need some intimate time with the Lord. You need to get up early to be with Him. You need to lay on your face before the Lord, letting God anoint you for His service, speaking whatever He tells you to say, and you do what He asks you to do.

Pray in your secret closet, letting the anointing break the yoke. Say: It's no more I, but the Christ that is within me. Ask God to impregnate you. Meet God early before anyone else gets up in the morning. Let Jesus know: You're the lover of my soul. Give Him a Hallelujah Praise, worship Him, and Spend time in His presence daily, asking for wisdom.

There is no birth from our lives until it is conceived. God impregnates us with the idea, with the gifts, with the talents, with the ministry. Picture it in your mind. Once an idea is conceived, the journey has to be made to complete the circle. The seed is already in you. It just needs to be brought forth and fertilized so that conception can take place.

Ask God for direction. Desire to be in the presence of God, to seek His direction, to know Him better. Be persistent in your prayer life. Learn and know who God really is. Asking for that wisdom and knowledge and understanding, knowing God more by reading His word. You will get to know

Him better when you constantly read His word. Proverbs 8:10-12 states:

> *Receive my instruction and not silver, and knowledge rather than choice gold. For wisdom is better than rubies, and all the things that may be desired are not to be compared to it. I, wisdom, dwell with prudence and find out knowledge of witty inventions. The fear of the Lord is to hate evil; pride and arrogance, and the evil way, and the forward mouth do I hate.*

Notes: Chapter 1

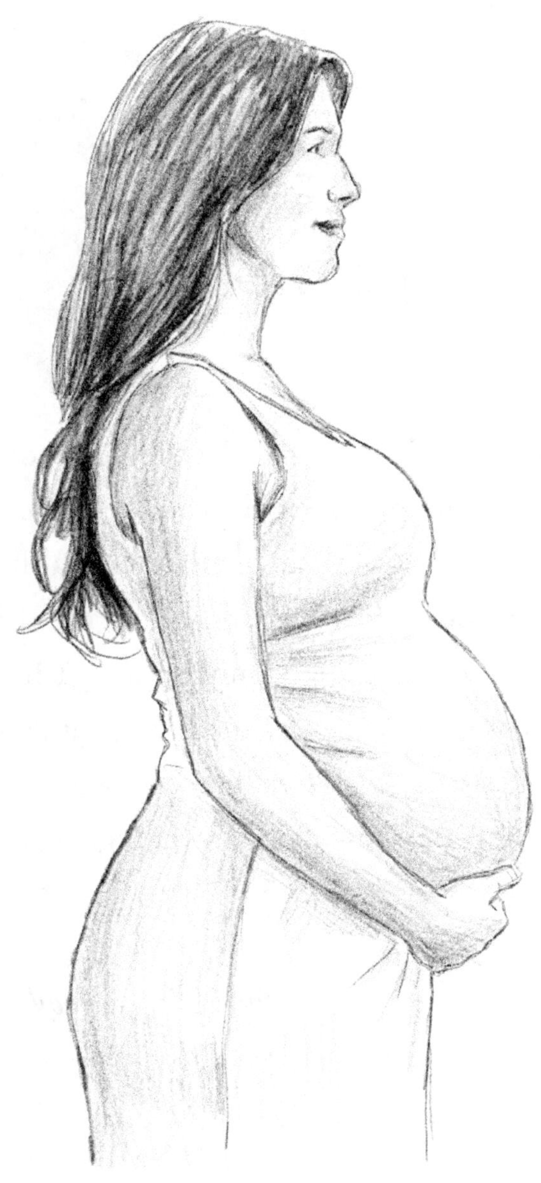

CHAPTER 2

I'm Pregnant

I'm pregnant! Oh, the excitement of being pregnant and preparing for your delivery. It's very important to promote nutritional health during your pregnancy. What is your soul and mind feasting on? Is it TV, social life, gambling, magazines, soap operas, gossiping or social media? Spiritually, what are you feasting on? Reading the word of God, praying and praising God, travailing, daily giving God all the glory. Psalms 34:8 says,

Taste and see that the LORD is good;
blessed is the one who takes refuge in
him.

Let's discuss your **Spiritual Nutrition Plan:** You need three meals and two snacks every day when you are pregnant.

1. Milk, cheese, yogurt – This looks like *PRAYER*. Pray without ceasing. (1 Thessalonians 5:17) and Giving Thanks - In everything give thanks: for this is the will of God in Christ Jesus concerning you. (1 Thessalonians 5:18)

2. Meat, poultry, fish, and proteins – This is *PRAISE*. (Psalms 150:6) Let everything that hath breath Praise the Lord, Praise ye the Lord!

3. Fruits – *PREPARE* (Galatians 5:22) The fruits of the spirit are: Love, Joy, Peace, Longsuffering, gentleness, goodness, faith, meekness, temperance.

4. Bread, cereal, pasta – *POSITION* (John 14:3) And if I go and prepare a place for you, I will come again, and receive you unto myself; that where I am, there you may be also.

5. Vegetables – *PROCLAIM* (Psalms 23:1) The Lord is my Shepherd; I shall not. (Psalms 34:1) I will bless the Lord at all times: his praise shall continually be in my mouth.

6. Liquids – WATER and Lots of fluids – PRESS (John 7:38) He that believeth on me, as the scripture hath said, out of his belly shall flow rivers of living water.

You need calories, proteins, fats, vitamins, fluids, and fiber. Spiritually, Get fat in Jesus. You will need to care for your spiritual life just like that infant in your womb, giving the Lord attention, adoration, and love.

Avoiding Spiritual Toxins

Avoid weight loss diets, caffeine, artificial sweeteners. Spiritually, this translates to people that aren't going anywhere, cliques in the church, negative people. Get with people going to the next level in God. The reason some of you have not birth what God has placed in your womb is because you want to stay with your friends, socializing, be part of the clique, gossiping, hang out with homegirls and going to parties, all because you want them to like you.

Are you fearful, or not sure what God wants you to do? Do you not want to go to the next level because your friends aren't going? Proverbs 3:5-6 advises:

> *"Trust in the Lord with all thine heart; and lean not unto thine own understanding. In all thine ways acknowledge him, and he shall direct your paths."*

Remember there is a friend that sticks closer than a brother. What a Friend we have in Jesus. Say to your friends: I got to do what God has predestined for me to do. God is calling me to do a work for Him and I'll go by myself without friends if I need to. I must progress, pray, praise, proclaim, position, prepare, and push.

The devil knows that if you deliver what's inside, you will start rebuking the devils on your job, at home, school, in the stores. You will be witnessing and ministering and going forth for God. Don't let distractions and life situations make you miscarriage or have premature birth or abortion.

Proverbs 8:10-12 repeats the importance of spiritual wisdom:

> *"Receive my instruction, and not silver; and knowledge rather than choice gold. For wisdom is better than rubies; and all the things that may be desired are not to be compared to it. I Wisdom dwell with prudence, and find out knowledge of witty inventions."*

Ask God for Wisdom, Knowledge and Understanding because you will need it for this journey. Yes, people will talk about you. Those are people that are BARREN. Their womb is closed. We must lay aside every weight and the sin, give up whatever endangers the relationship with God and run this race. Keep our eyes off ourselves and the circumstances that surround us. Stop worrying about what people think or how they feel. We are running for the Lord.

In 2 Chronicles 20:15—we see a biblical promise encouraging us to trust God, let Him fight our battles, instead of trying to win with your own strength:

"The battle is not yours, but the Lord's."

Psalms 34:1 says:

"I will bless the Lord at all times."

Matthew 6:33-34 encourages,

"But seek first his kingdom and his righteousness, and all these things will be given to you as well. Therefore, do not worry about tomorrow, for

tomorrow will worry about itself. Each day has enough trouble of its own."

Notes: Chapter 2

15

Stages of Labor

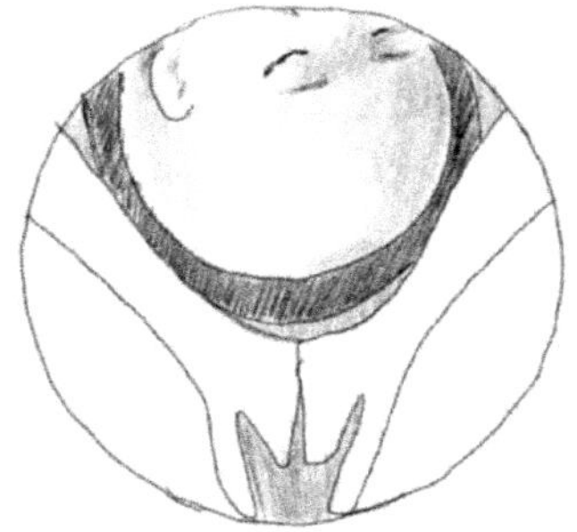

Latent Stage (0 – 3 centimeters)

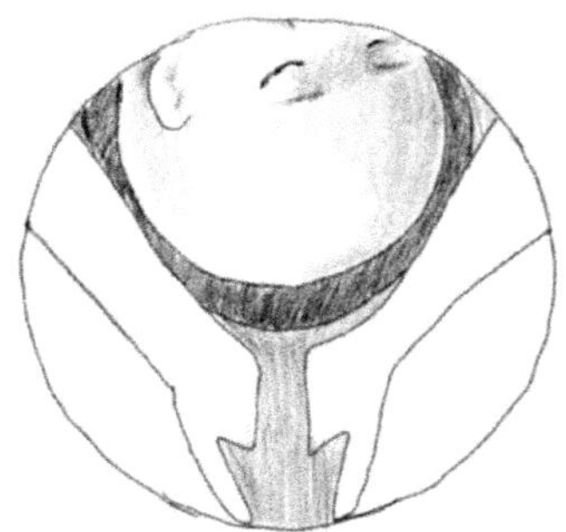

Active Stage (4 – 7 centimeters)

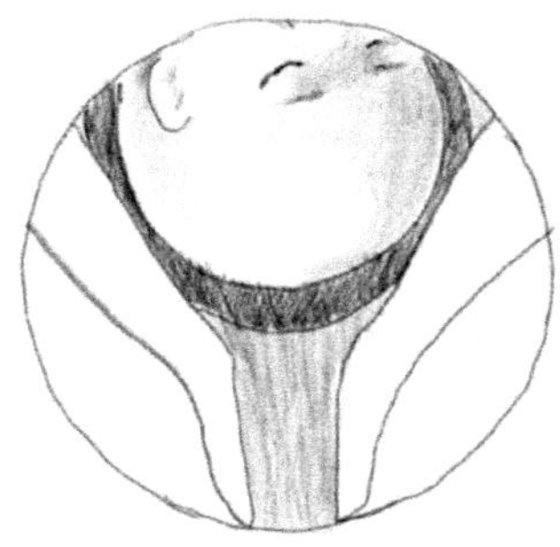

Molding Stage (8 – 10 centimeters)

CHAPTER 3

Labor & Travail

Welcome to labor on your way to delivery. You are about to give birth to your Destiny, Gifts, Talents, Dreams, and Vision. The spiritual birthing experience parallels the physical stages of labor and delivery starting with:

The Sounds of Labor

Jeremiah 4:31 states:

"I heard a cry as of a woman in labor, a groan as of one bearing her first child—the cry of the daughter of

Zion, gasping for breath, stretching out her hands and saying, I am fainting; my life is given over to murderers."

In the delivery room, you will hear medical terms that reflect spiritual stages such as:

● *No pain, no labor*

These are referred to as "Braxton Hicks contractions." It is contractions which do not increase in intensity or frequency. This is known as false labor. All you need to do is change your position, get some rest. and drink plenty of water.

● *Pain with labor*

That's travailing to bring forth.

● *Ripening*

This is where the cervix becomes butter-soft and tips forward signaling the labor is close.

● *Show*

Here, the mucus plug and blood appear. This parallels with Jesus, the Savior who suffered, bled, and died for us.

Components of Labor (The Four P's)

1. *Passage* (a woman's pelvis): Your vessel for God's glory.
2. *Passenger* (the fetus): Your position and presentation. I'll go Lord; however, whenever, and whatever you require.
3. *Power* (uterine contractions): Your prayer life, praise, and anointing. The Holy Spirit is in control (Acts 1:8).

4. *Psyche* (woman's psyche is preserved afterwards): She can view this as a positive experience, excited, in awe, increased self-esteem, and confidence. Don't lose your praise and don't forget God.

The normal presentation is vertex (head first). This means you must protect your mind. Your mind, or brain, is very important to the human body. You have to protect your head.

As a Christian you must stand firm with the helmet of salvation. Don't let the devil get a hold of your mind. He wants to destroy your relationship with God so you must protect your mind and your brain. It's the brain that operates the body. It controls and coordinates all body functions including your movements, emotions, memory, and thoughts.

"Do not conform to the pattern of this world, but be transformed by the renewing of your mind. Then you will be able to test and approve what

God's will is—his good, pleasing and perfect will."

Romans 12:2 NIV

The Stages of Labor (Dilating to 10 cm)

There are three stages involved with labor. In the natural, a physician makes sure you are checked regularly to see how far along you have moved and in making sure progress is being made toward your delivery. From the time your water burst, they like to have the baby delivered in twenty-four hours.

God knows your process and how long you are to be in each stage concerning bringing forth your destiny. He doesn't want you to deliver before you are ready nor does He want you to keep it in longer than you should. The term used to express how far one is moving along is dilating. This is part of the process. Dilating has to do with the expansion needed to bring to birth what God has put in you. Let's look at these stages involved with the labor.

- ***Latent Stage*** *(0 to 4 centimeters)*: This is the first stage of labor. Naturally, you're looking and smelling good, talking on the phone, laughing, and visitors are in the room. Spiritually, you're going to church, hitting and missing, skipping tithing. It's a social thing with you.

- ***Active Stage*** *(4 to 7 centimeters)*: Your membranes are ruptured for amniotic fluid to escape. Spiritually, this is when you're saying, Purge me, God. If you find anything that should not be in my life, take it out. Turn the spotlight of heaven on my soul.

The pain increases at this point. You're starting to pray more and listen to the voice of God, having dreams and visions, hungry and thirsty after righteousness. I'm ready to do what God wants. Naturally, the baby has been pushing on your bladder, stomach, bowels, and diaphragm for months. I can't wait to deliver this baby.

At this point, the power of the Holy Spirit is needed, oxytocin (pitocin) is given intravenously to help contract the uterus, increasing the power of the contraction. The main focus is delivering what God has impregnated you with.

While we call it labor, the Bible calls it travailing. It is a time of painful or laborious effort. It's hard work, intense suffering, and the hardships associated with the physical agony of child birth or mental and spiritual struggle against the evil of the world.

- ***Molding Stage*** *(around 8 centimeters)*: You start asking people to leave at this point. People don't understand what is happening to you. Your hair is all over the head. You are crying and screaming with your contractions as the baby moves down the canal.

You have molding happening with destiny inside you. These are the changes in the shape of the fetus skull. Spiritually, God is molding you for the job. He is doing it His way, not yours. You are saying, "You are the potter Lord, and I am the clay.

Mold me, Lord for your service. God have thine own way in my life.

> *"I praise you because I am fearfully*
> *and wonderfully made; your works*
> *are wonderful, I know that full well."*
>
> *Psalms 139:14*

Notes: Chapter 3

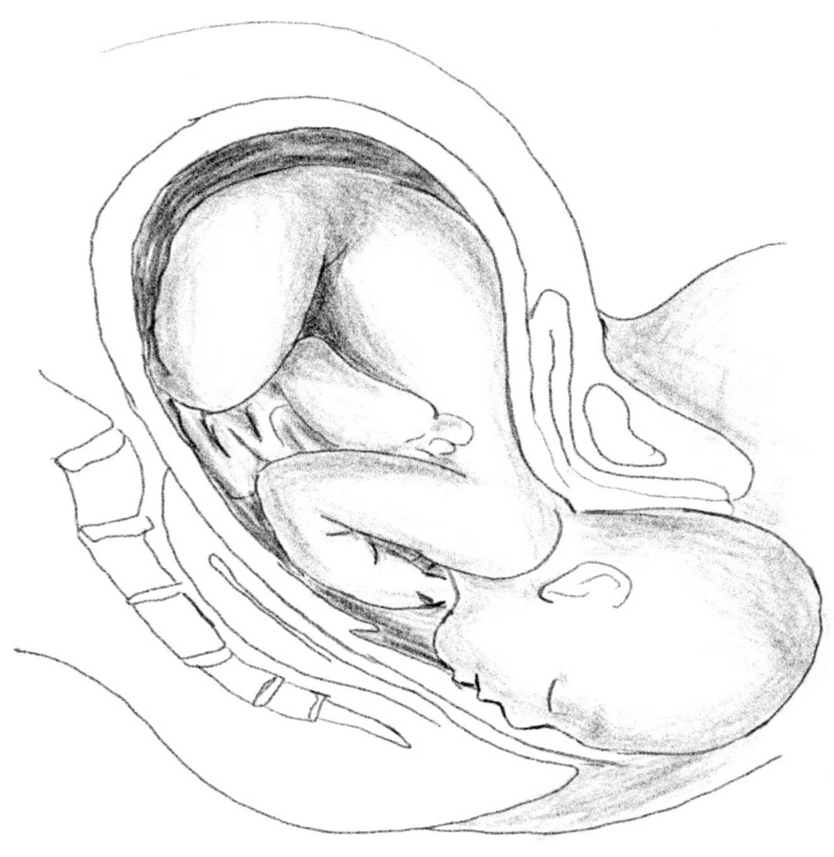

The Natural Birth

CHAPTER 4

Time for Delivery

We are now so close to seeing our dream in fruition. So close to seeing the fulfillment of what we have been anticipating for so long. This is not the time to get comfortable or relax, but rather to exert the needed strength to get over the very last hurdle.

You are fully dilated. This means your cervix has expanded to the necessary size of ten centimeters, enabling the delivery. This is your crowning moment. Your baby's head becomes somewhat visible at the opening. This is the time to push. Spiritually speaking as well, the manifestation of what God has impregnated you with is here.

It's time to push with all your might; with everything you have. You have an overwhelming, uncontrollable urge to push or to bear down with the contractions. You have reached a point that you can't hold back pushing down when those contractions happen. You are about to deliver.

When it's delivery time, there are six movements that must happen. These are called the Six Cardinal Movements. The cardinal movements during the last part of labor is where the fetus must reposition, making changes and turns necessary to become an overcomer and get the baby out. They are as follows:

1. *Descent—* **prayer.**
2. *Flexion—***praise.**
3. *Internal rotation—***position.**
4. *Extension—***prepare.**
5. *External rotation—***proclaim.**
6. *Expulsion ---- **PRESS***

(The baby is out. He pushes himself
out, or we help him to come out.

That is PRESS (Pressing your way through).

During labor, sometimes you have to reach over, grab your husband's hand or your mama's hand; whoever is there with you. Hold my hand while I push. And if you don't have anyone there, the nurse will hold your hand. Let's push. You are pushing with every contraction. Sometimes you might have to ask your Sisters, Pastor, First Lady, Ministers, Deacons to pray and hold hands with you. Matthews 18:19 says,

> *"If two of you shall agree on earth as touching anything that they shall ask, it shall be done for them of my Father which is in heaven."*

Overcoming Obstacles and Delivery

There are situations in life and distractions which can cause miscarriage, prematurity, and abortions. Sometimes we cannot get the baby out by the birth canal, but never worry. Regardless of whatever happens, ***DO NOT LET THE DEVIL STOP YOUR BIRTH!*** Don't let him block or reroute the plan that God has prepared for you. Sometimes you will have to say, "God, whatever way you can bless me, I'll be satisfied."

The enemy will try a ***breech*** with your dream. With a pregnancy and delivery, this means a baby is attempting to come out feet first instead of head first. This is dangerous and a high risk for both the dream carrier (mother) and the destiny (child). However, God always has a ram in the bush. He has provided your answer. Your next step would be a C-section (cutting your abdomen open). No matter how hard the enemy fights, you must never let him take your dream away. Bring it to birth despite the fact. **Remember, you can do all things through Christ.** He gives you the strength.

Notes: Chapter 4

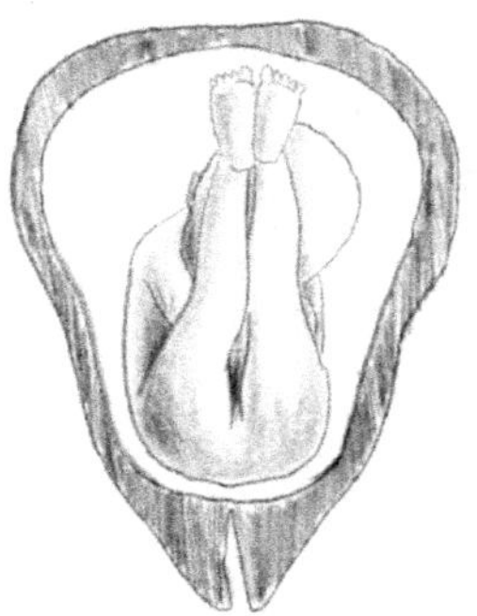

Frank Breach

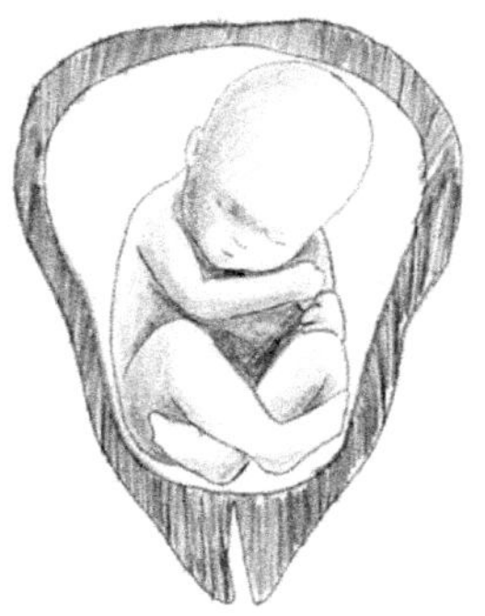

Complete Breach

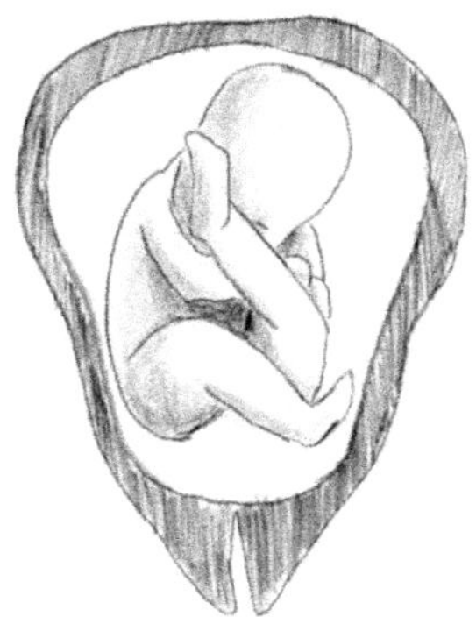

Footling Breech

CHAPTER 5

Nursing Destiny

Baby Destiny has arrived and your job is still far from being over. As much as it took to bring him forth, his debut to the rest of the world requires continual support. The goal is for whatever God has birthed out of you, to stay as healthy as possible.

After the infant is out of the womb, he is placed under the incubator with nurses caring for him and keeping the infant warm. We are checking and looking, making sure respiration and heart rate is good as we are cleaning the body of the baby. The baby is wrapped with a warm blanket and given to the mother to bond, and have skin to skin contact, with kisses and hugs showing love and affection.

Once the baby is out of the womb, breathing on his own, he starts moving his head, tongue, and lips searching for nourishment. The need for milk is a natural instinct for a baby.

As a nurse and mother, I encourage breast feeding. It provides numerous advantages such as good nutrition, immune system support, lowering the risk of certain diseases, and other benefits. Also, it helps the mother to recover faster, and promotes mother and baby bonding.

> *"Like newborn babies, crave pure spiritual milk, so that by it you may grow up in your salvation, now that you have tasted that the Lord is good."*
>
> *1 Peter 2:2-3 NIV*

Spiritually, milk is the Word of God. After birthing your gift, talents, ministry, or knowing what God has given you to do, you will find nourishment in God's Word. Once we see our need for God's Word, and how we are growing and maturing in the

Lord, our appetite leads us to drink more milk so our body, soul, and mind are well nourished.

Have you noticed how you are growing? How strong is your desire for God's Word? Do you desire to birth destiny, to lean and depend on God and obey His Word? To be still and know that He is God?

We must spend time with God, engage in prayer, and study the Bible to stay connected with God. We must not forget to praise, pray, give adoration, and lift up the name of the Lord daily. Bless the name of the Lord! We are more than conquerors!

Romans 8:37 NIV says,

> *"No, in all these things we are more than conquerors through him who loved us."*

Notes: Chapter 5

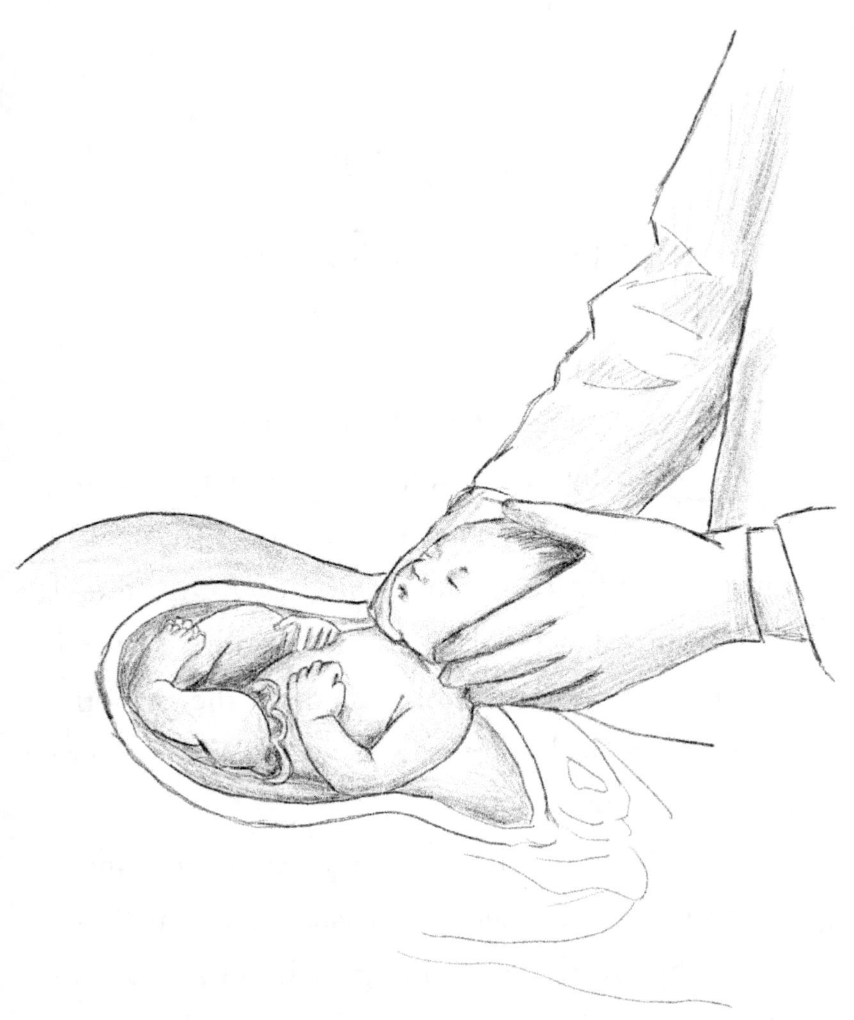

C-section delivery

CHAPTER 6

Stewarding Destiny

As discussed in the last chapter, when a baby is born, it is customary (barring an emergency that requires immediate intervention for the infant or mother) for the infant to be immediately placed at the mother's breast. For the first time, the mother beholds the gift—the blessing—to feel and assess it, to hear it cry with every ounce of its being.

The baby is ushered into a new environment where it must immediately sustain its own life—mainly by breathing—harking back to the moment of man's creation, when God breathed the breath of life into the human (Genesis 2:7). The infant is placed at its mother's breast for warmth, consolation, and soothing, to be calmed and to adjust to its new surroundings.

The birthing of your destiny carries a similar responsibility: once it is given, you must usher it into existence, providing the focus for its promise. However, Destiny must first be offered back to God, for it never belonged to its bearer in the first place. **YOUR DESTINY MUST BE SURRENDERED TO GOD.**

Mary will tell you that she was chosen to be a mother through supernatural means, but the Savior of the world was not hers to keep. Yes, Jesus was her child, but most importantly, He was our Savior—the promised Messiah.

If you for one moment think your destiny belongs to you, you are mistaken. It's probably intended for your business, your ministry, your family, an unsaved or wayward child—for the world. Herein lies the rub, so let me make it personal: Your wealth, your child, your business, your job, your ministry does not belong to you—they are the Lord's.

We see, from the example of Hannah, she was barren and desired to bear a child more than anything. Her humanistic desire to have a child was canceled out by her sacrificial offering. Although her desperation originated from a selfish place, her desire to give the child back unselfishly to the Lord superseded her own needs. She understood better than most that the destiny she birthed was for the Lord.

After she had nursed and weaned him, she surrendered the destiny—her son, Samuel—to Eli the priest. Notice that she first had to nurse him with milk, to care for him with her hands, to clean, to sing, and to instruct him in the most modest of means. This illustrates that we, too, must facilitate the same methods of maturing what God has given us, remembering that even though we may plant and water, God gives the growth (1 Corinthians 3:6).

The journey that began with a vision and a planting, through the carrying and birthing, must now be prepped for its final mission—its destiny. Just as a righteous person is like a tree planted by streams of water that yields its fruit in season (Psalm 1:3), our destiny must be nurtured and rooted in God to be truly fruitful.

Remember, we must be careful what we sow, because whatever one sows, that will he also reap (Galatians 6:7). This means the preparation we put into our destiny determines its harvest. In Samuel's case, his destiny included: warning the children of Israel against their desire to have a King; standing before a King (Saul) and letting him know that God had removed him due to disobedience; and secretly anointing a shepherd boy named David as the next king.

Romans 12:6-21 says,

> *"We have different gifts, according to the grace given to each of us. If your gift is prophesying, then prophesy in accordance with your faith; if it is serving, then serve; if it is teaching, then teach; if it is to encourage, then give encouragement; if it is giving, then give generously; if it is to lead, do it diligently; if it is to show mercy, do it cheerfully.*

Love must be sincere. Hate what is evil; cling to what is good. Be devoted to one another in love. Honor one another above yourselves. Never be lacking in zeal, but keep your spiritual fervor, serving the Lord.

Be joyful in hope, patient in affliction, faithful in prayer. Share with the Lord's people who are in need. Practice hospitality. Bless those who persecute you; bless and do not curse. Rejoice with those who rejoice; mourn with those who mourn. Live in harmony with one another. Do not be proud, but be willing to associate with people of low position. Do not be conceited. Do not repay anyone evil for evil. Be careful to do what is right in the eyes of everyone.

If it is possible, as far as it depends on you, live at peace with everyone. Do not take revenge, my dear friends, but leave room for God's wrath, for it is written: "It is mine to avenge; I will repay," says the Lord. On the contrary: "If your enemy is hungry, feed him; if he is thirsty, give him something to drink. In doing this, you will heap burning coals on his head." "Do not be overcome by evil, but overcome evil with good."

Notes: Chapter 6

The **UMBILICAL CORD** is a flexible tube that supplies oxygen and nutrients to the fetus during pregnancy and removes waste.

The **PLACENTA** is a temporary organ that is developed in the uterus during the pregnancy for a life support system. Inside, it connects the fetus to the mother to provide oxygen and nutrients to the fetus. Within 30 minutes of the baby being birthed, the placenta is delivered out through a uterine contraction.

WORD FROM GOD

God is saying, I was monitoring your progress for nine months as you go from one level to the next, one centimeter to ten centimeters: I have watched your: vital signs (blood pressure, respiration, pulse, oxygen), lab tests (blood sugars, electrolytes, complete blood counts), sonograms (good fluid levels), Assess uterine contractions, Checked; Pelvis adequacy and monitoring the fetus, making sure nothing came between you and Me because you are Mine, I love you with a everlasting love.

I don't change, I don't lie and every promise in the Book is yours. The umbilical cord connects the developing fetus to the mother's placenta, serving as a lifeline for nutrients, oxygen and blood. The placenta holds wisdom and knowledge, also the hurts, the pain, the knocks and the bumps, which make you better, keeps you humble. It is ugly looking, but it was what supplied the food and the blood to your baby. If the placenta detaches itself from you, the baby will die. Listen, God is your life support. There is nothing like the blood of Jesus.

I advise you to push. Push until something happens. Don't give up. Don't give out. Because God is there. He is your helper. He has promised this in many places in the Bible. He promises:

> *"The LORD himself goes before you and will be with you; he will never leave you nor forsake you. Do not be afraid; do not be discouraged."*

> *Deuteronomy 31:8*

Get up and do it. Don't let fear keep you from doing what God has given you to do. Don't let fear and people talking distract you from doing whatever God has assigned you to do. **Get up and be about your Father's business. GOD needs you to birth!**

We have to be ready like Mary, the mother of Jesus, when the angel Gabriel brought news to her saying, "You will become pregnant, give birth, have a son, and name him Jesus. He will be great and called the Son of God Most High." She answered, "I am a virgin, I'm getting married, how is this going to happen?" After God spoke to her, Mary said, "Behold the handmaid of the Lord; be it unto me according to your word." (Luke 1:26-38). God's will, is always going to be done.

To all of my older brothers and sisters: Don't get rid of the crib, you have another baby inside of you. Spiritually, what is your gifts and talents, your purpose, your ministry? Isaiah 66:8-11 powerfully concludes:

> *"Who has ever heard of such a thing?*
> *Who has ever seen such things? Can a*
> *country be born in a day or a nation*
> *be brought forth in a moment? Yet no*
> *sooner is Zion in labor than she gives*
> *birth to her children.* ***Do I bring to***
> ***the moment of birth and not give***

delivery? *says the Lord. Do I close up the womb when I bring to delivery? says your God."*

"Rejoice with Jerusalem and be glad for her, all you who love her; rejoice greatly with her, all you who mourn over her. **For you will nurse and be satisfied** *at her comforting breast; you will drink deeply and delight in her overflowing abundance. For this is what the Lord says."*

God, impregnate your people with the seed of your Word. Don't let them abort that dream, ministry, their talents or visions, but carry it all to full term and birth it. PUSH!!!

"Before she goes into labor, she gives birth; before the pains come upon her, she delivers a son. Who has ever

heard of such things? Who has ever seen things like this? Can a country be born in a day or a nation be brought forth in a moment? Yet no sooner is Zion in labor than she gives birth to her children."

"Do I bring to the moment of birth and not give delivery?" says the Lord. *"Do I close up the womb when I bring to delivery?" says your God. "Rejoice with Jerusalem and be glad for her, all you who love her; rejoice greatly with her, all you who mourn over her. For you will nurse and be satisfied at her comforting breasts; you will drink deeply and delight in her overflowing abundance."*

Isaiah 66:7-11

Notes

A PRAYER FOR DESTINY

Praises to our Lord God,
Hallelujah to our Heavenly Father.
Lord, I adore You; You are great and mighty
and worthy of all praise.
You are good. Thank You for new mercies every day.
Thank You, Jesus, for dying on the cross for us.

You created us, God, in Your image and likeness.
You have a plan and a purpose for our life.
Your kingdom come, your will be done
Thank You for Your power, Your presence,
and Your promises in our lives.

Lord, I'm asking for favor!
You Lord have never failed me yet.
God, impregnate Your people, your soldiers,
missionaries, preachers, disciples, prophets, and laborers.
You said Lord,
"The harvest is plentiful, but the laborers are few."
We realize there is a great need for a task to be done,
but not enough people to do it. (Matthew 9:37)

I'm asking you God to impregnate them
with the seed of Your Word.
Don't let them abort their dream, ministry, vision,
or talent, but carry it to full term and birth it.
I pray and encourage each person to
PUSH Until Something Happens
In Jesus Name I Pray. AMEN

Linda Dorothy Talley is first and foremost a woman of God. She loves God and people and has given her life to serving and helping others with a heart of love and the gift of helps.

She received her Bachelor's degree in nursing and public health nursing [PHN] from the University of Phoenix. She has been in the medical profession for over 56 years as an LVN and Registered Nurse, working in every field of nursing: emergency nursing care, maternity special care, postpartum, labor and delivery, and Lamaze instructing. She is a qualified, specialty certified obstetrician.

She is also a church mother and district missionary for the Fourth Jurisdiction COGIC, reaching out and speaking to numerous women locally and nationally. She is a mother to so many, besides her own children, grand, and great-grandchildren. She resides in Southern California.

Author Contact: pushdot1949@yahoo.com